Contents

Muchelney Road, London 1931

New houses

"Our house cost £450. We put £25 down as a deposit and paid off 11 shillings (55p) **a week for 25 years."**

New Malden, Surrey 1930

This house was built in 1930. It is joined to the house next door. It is a semi-detached house.

Look for:

— the front door with a long glass panel
— the casement windows with metal frames
— the pattern of sunrays on the gate
— the cement walls of the house. Cement has been put over the bricks. This is called cement rendering. Sometimes the builders threw small stones on to wet cement. Then they called it pebble dash.

The first council houses were built in the 1930s. Sometimes they were built round a large square of grass.

"Council houses were only rented to families with children. The children played on the grass patch between each row."

St. Helier Estate, London 1934

Things to do

Start a book of your own about life *At home in the 1930s.*

Find some houses near where you live that were built in the 1930s. Look for clues like cement rendering, pebble dash walls, sunray patterns and casement windows that open outwards. Draw pictures or take photographs of the houses. Stick them in your book.

The family

Families were not very large in the 1930s. Most parents had one or two children. Look at the two photographs. Look carefully at the clothes they are wearing and their hair styles.

Woodford, Essex 1934

"Women wore calf length dresses with art-silk stockings and button shoes. Everyone wanted their hair waved as perms had just been invented. I had mine done just before I got married."

Both the fathers are wearing three-piece suits.
Their hair is cut very short.

"We went to the barber every fortnight."

"We had to wear short trousers until we were 12 or 13 years old, even in the winter."

In this photograph, the younger boy is wearing a romper suit knitted by his mother. The older boy has a jacket and trousers made of grey flannel, grey knitted socks and lace up shoes. His hair is short too.

Venn brothers

Things to do

Talk to someone older than 60 who can tell you what life was like in the 1930s. Ask them about their home and family. Where did they live? What size was their family? What clothes did they wear? Write down what they tell you in your book.

Try to find some family snapshots that were taken in the 1930s.

Electricity

"We were very pleased when we bought our house because it included all the fittings. We had gas and electricity all through the house."

In the 1930s most houses had electricity for the first time. Electric light was the greatest improvement. The two people in the photograph could read in the evening, even though it was dark outside and the curtains were drawn.

There are three kinds of electric light in the sitting room in the photograph.
Look for:

— the ceiling light
— the wall light
— the standard lamp.

"I remember the first electric iron I had. I had to put one shilling (5p) **in the meter when I wanted to use it."**

Houses with electricity were called "labour saving" homes. Household equipment that worked from electricity made the housework easier.

This electric fire and vacuum cleaner were very modern in the 1930s. Now they are in a museum.

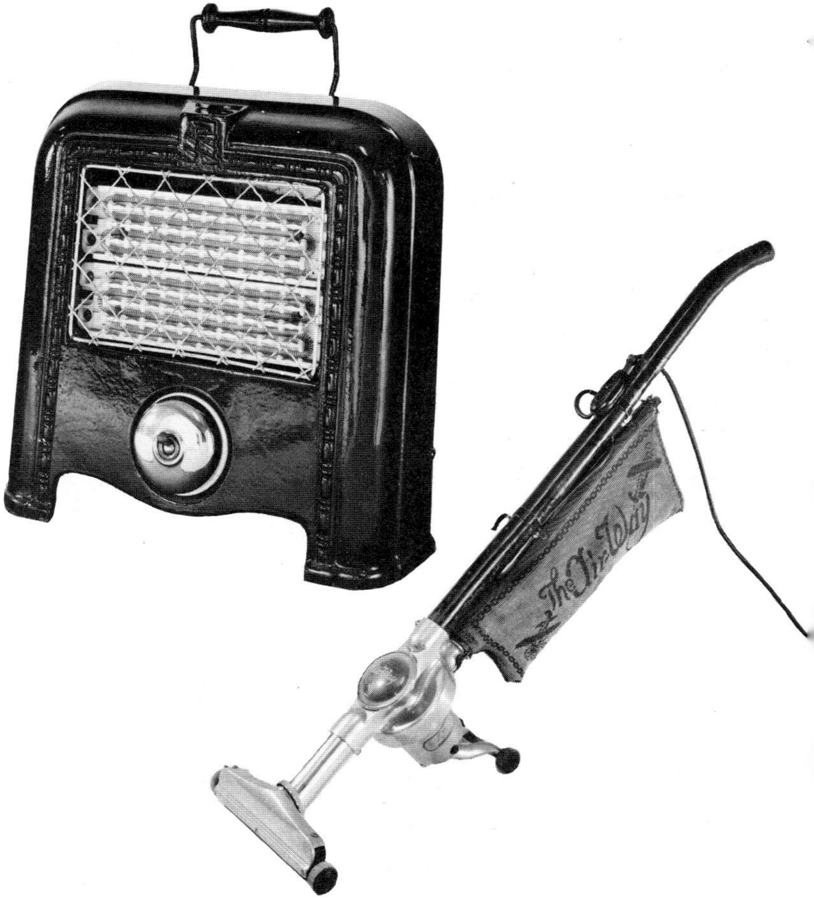

Things to do

Draw a picture of someone using the 1930s vacuum cleaner. Look at the vacuum cleaner in your home, if you have one. How is it different from the one in the photograph?

Talk to someone older than 60 about the first time they used electricity. How did it make life easier for them? Write down what they tell you in your book.

Gas

"We didn't even have to buy a cooker but hired one from the Gas Board for one shilling (5p) **a week."**

Gas was cheaper than electricity. Most people used it for cooking and for heating water.

This man is using a gas cooker to boil the water in his kettle. Look for:

— the gas taps to turn on the gas
— the grill pan for making toast
— the plate rack to warm plates.

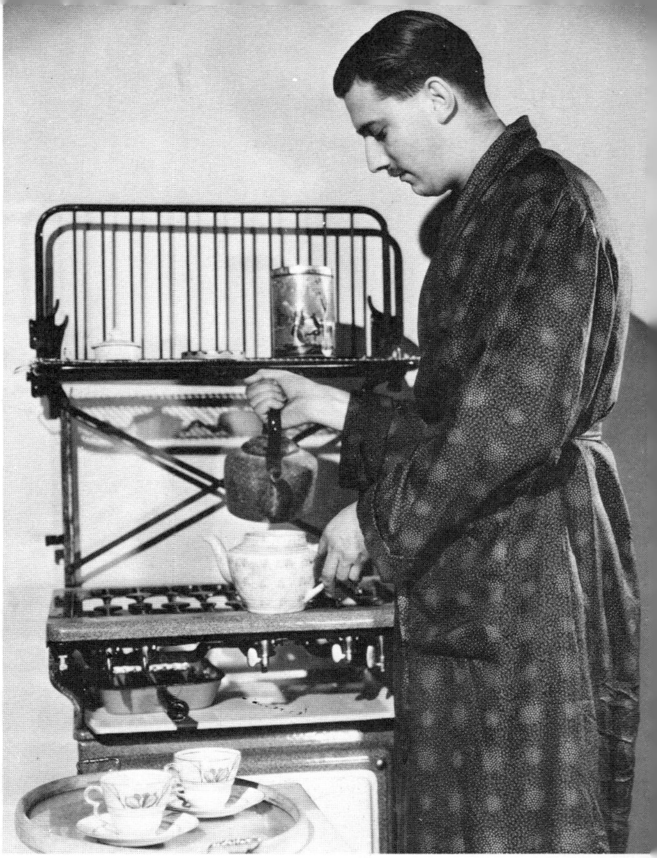

Some kitchens in the 1930s had a gas geyser as one of the fittings. When lit, it heated water for the hot water taps. You can see one over the sink in this newspaper advertisement.

Water for the washing was heated in a gas boiler like the one in the photograph.

"I filled it with water from the cold tap, lit the gas and waited for the water to heat up. Then I put in the dirty clothes and moved the handle backwards and forwards to wash them. I took the clothes out with a copper stick and put them through the wringer into the sink. Then I emptied the water out through the tap at the bottom."

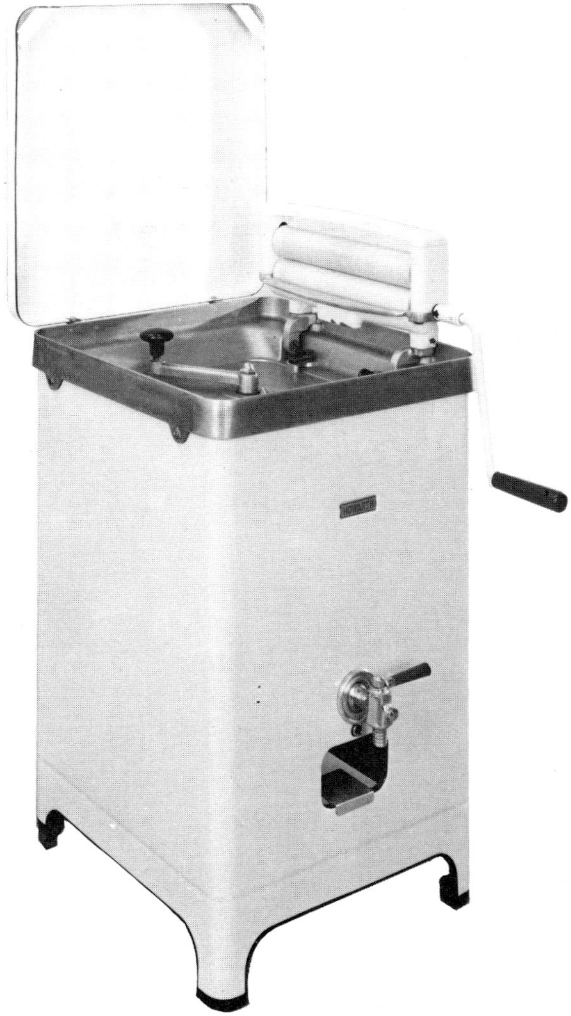

Things to do

In your book, draw a picture of a "labour saving" kitchen in the 1930s. Put in some things that used gas and some that used electricity.

In the 1930s, gas was made from coal at the Gas Works. Where does the gas we use in our homes today come from?

Coal fires

Tiger Bay, Cardiff, Wales 1939

There was no central heating at home in the 1930s.
The family kept themselves warm by sitting round the fire.

"I used to light the dining room fire in the morning, let it go out and light the sitting room fire in the afternoon."

Some fireplaces had a boiler behind them to heat the water.
Some families boiled a saucepan on the fire too. Look for the saucepans on the fire in the photograph.

"Every morning I cleared out the ash from the fire of the day before. Then I refilled the coal scuttle with coal from the coal store outside the back door."

Darwen, Lancashire

This coal scuttle has a galleon carved on it. This was a popular pattern in the 1930s.

Look for the coal scuttle in this picture. It is being used as a stool.

Things to do

In your book write about heating the home in the 1930s.

Ask someone older than 60 if they have their old coal scuttle.

Look out for a galleon picture on houses and furniture from the 1930s. Some houses had a galleon picture of coloured glass in the front door.

Afternoon tea

Bermondsey, London 1932

"We went into the sitting room on Sundays or if we had somebody coming to tea."

When visitors came to tea, the best tea service and best tablecloth were used. Cakes were put on a cakestand. Sugar lumps were served, using sugar tongs.

"My mother's friends kept their hats on and sometimes their gloves as well."

Look at these pictures of best bone china tea sets. The china was so thin you could see your fingers through it. Look for:

— the shape of the cups, plate and jugs
— the hand-painted patterns
— the lump sugar and sugar tongs
— the slop basin. Tea leaves left at the bottom of a cup were put into this before another cup of tea was poured.

Things to do

Talk to someone older than 60 about afternoon tea parties. Write down what they tell you in your book.

Draw a picture of people having afternoon tea in the 1930s.

Look in an antique shop or on a market stall for hand-painted china from the 1930s. Ask an old person you know if they have a best tea service from the 1930s.

Upstairs

"The house had a nice little bathroom and three bedrooms. Even in the small bedroom, I could get in a wardrobe and single bed."

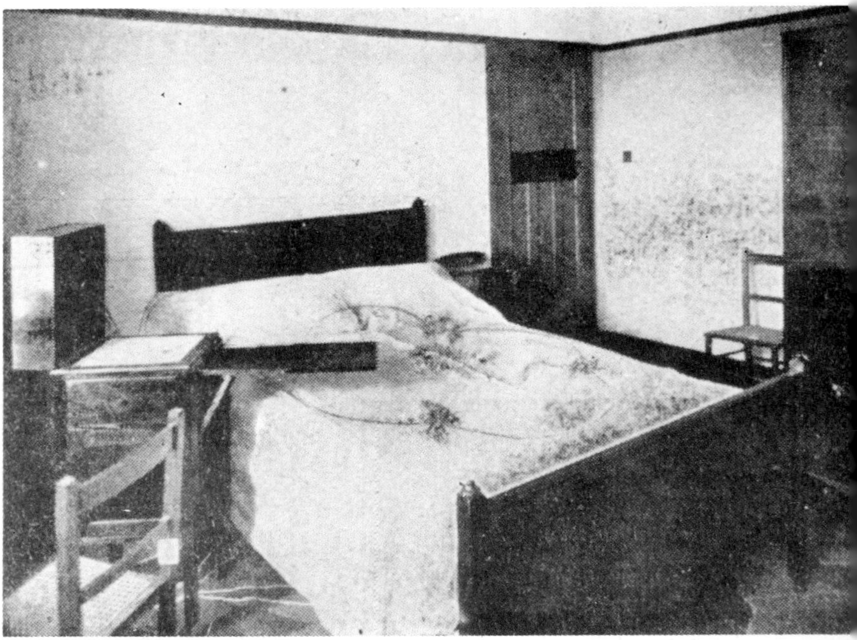

Hurst Park Avenue, Cambridge 1930

The bedroom furniture often took up the whole room. The beds had wooden headboards and footboards. The wardrobes were large and heavy. Most dressing tables had three swinging mirrors.

Heald Green, Ches

"My bedroom suite was the most expensive suite in the house. £20 it cost. Every week I polished it with wax polish until it shone like glass."

Some bedrooms had a fireplace. A fire was lit if someone was ill or to keep a baby warm. This baby is having a bath in front of the fire.

This bathroom was very up to date.
Look for:

- the tiled wall
- the lino on the floor
- the white porcelain bath and basin
- the gas geysers by the bath and basin
- the towel rail on the right.

Not all bathrooms were as grand as this one.

"Our bathroom was tiny. When you got out of the bath it was difficult to find a space to dry yourself."

In some houses the toilet was in the bathroom.
In other houses, it was outside the back door.

Things to do

Look upstairs in a house that was built in the 1930s. Are there fireplaces in the bedrooms? Are there any geysers in the bathroom?

Draw a picture of a bedroom with all its furniture.

Find out how much a bedroom suite costs now.

Outside

Elmer Gardens, Isleworth, London

"When we moved here in 1930, there were cornfields at the back of us."

New housing estates were built on the outskirts of the town. The streets were called the suburbs. All the houses had front and back gardens.

"We had a bit of lawn and then a vegetable garden. There was a corner piece with trees and shrubs. We built a rockery with stone and concrete."

Families enjoyed themselves in the garden. They took many snapshots there.

"I was always out in the garden or on the allotment. I grew all our vegetables and if I had any spare money I'd put it by for a packet of seeds."

The allotment was a piece of land not far from the housing estate, where families grew food to eat. They saved a lot of money that way.

Things to do

Look carefully at family snapshots taken in the 1930s.
How many were taken in the garden?

Write down some of the things people did in their gardens.

Draw a picture of a family on their allotment digging up vegetables.

Luxuries

This house has a garage and separate garage gates.
The owners are washing their car outside on the pavement.
Their car is a Morris 8 and cost £100. They did not use it to go to work, but for holidays or short drives into the country.

"Cars were a great luxury and there weren't many about in 1930. We went about on our bicycles or had things delivered by a horse and cart."

Not many people had a telephone at home. This one has a mouthpiece to speak into and a receiver which you lift off its hook. This connected you to the operator at the telephone exchange.

"When you lifted the receiver the operator answered. She usually chatted about the weather before saying, 'Number please' and connected you to the person you wanted to speak to."

Things to do

Collect some pictures of old cars.

Talk to someone older than 60 who remembers riding in a 1930s car. Write down what they tell you.

Make up a play with two friends about a telephone conversation in the 1930s. Phone somebody up and ask them to come to afternoon tea. One friend must be the telephone operator, the other the person you want to invite.

Children's amusements

Above: Whitefield, Manchester

There were toys to play with inside and outside. Look at the children on their toy cars and tricycle.

Some toys came in boxes, like this clockwork train set.

"Every birthday I got another set of Meccano. I made models on the dining room table and they really worked."

Some children had a weekly comic or looked at *Children's Corner* in the newspaper.

"There was *Comic Cuts* and *Chips* with Tired Tim and Weary Willie."

Collecting was popular, especially cigarette cards, bus tickets, stamps and coins.

"I swapped cigarette cards with my friends at school until I had the set I wanted."

Things to do

Talk to someone older than 60 about children's toys and games in the 1930s. Find out the names of cartoon characters from that time. How many of these can be seen in comics today?

Look out for collections of cigarette cards in second hand shops or jumble sales.

Family entertainment

"Everyone wanted a wireless set."

Electricity at home helped to provide family entertainment. Children listened to Children's Hour at 5.00 pm each day. They came to know the voices of these four people well.

Ekco 1934

Elizabeth, Stephen, 'Mac' and Barbara 1934

Adults listened to comedy shows, popular songs, talks and dance bands.

"Gracie Fields, Elsie and Doris Waters, and Arthur Askey were some of the stars. I liked hearing Billy Cotton and Henry Hall with their bands. Henry Hall always ended the programme with 'Here's to the next time'."

Many people wanted to sing the radio "hits" at home, playing the tunes on their piano. Here are some of the words of one of them:

> "Red sails in the sunset
> Way out on the sea,
> Oh, carry my loved one
> Home safely to me."

Things to do

Find someone who can sing you the tune of "Red Sails in the Sunset".

Ask someone older than 60 which radio programmes and radio stars they listened to in the 1930s. Write down what they tell you.

Look out for cigarette card collections which show some of the radio stars of the 1930s.

"Before the war"

The Second World War began on 3 September 1939. When people talk about a time "before the war", they are talking about the 1930s. It is more than 50 years ago.

How has life at home changed since then?

London 1939

The following museums collect and display things about life at home in the 1930s:

The Geffrye Museum, Kingsland Road, Shoreditch, London
The Museum of London, London Wall
Castle Museum, Tower Street, York
North of England Open Air Museum, Beamish Hall, Stanley, County Durham
The Science Museum, Exhibition Road, South Kensington, London
Museum of Childhood, High Street, Edinburgh, Scotland
